what the Bible
has to say about:

money

ISBN 0-687-07552-1

Scripture quotations are taken from the HOLY BIBLE, NEW
INTERNATIONAL VERSION ®. Copyright © 1973, 1978, 1984
International Bible Society.

Original edition published in English under the title
What God Has to Say About: Money by John Hunt Publishing Ltd,
New Alresford, Hants, UK.

This book was conceived, designed, and produced by

THE PALM PRESS
The Old Candlemakers, West Street
Lewes, East Sussex BN7 2NZ, UK

Creative Director: PETER BRIDGEWATER
Publisher: SOPHIE COLLINS
Editorial Director: STEVE LUCK
Designer: ANDREW MILNE
Project Editor: MANDY GREENFIELD

03 04 05 06 07 08 09 10 11 12 — 10 9 8 7 6 5 4 3 2 1

Manufactured in China

Introduction "When I was young I thought that money was the most important thing in life," said Oscar Wilde; "now that I am old I know it is."

People laugh because of the surprise ending: you would expect Oscar Wilde to have learned wisdom in his old age. But many also have a feeling that he may be right, and then feel guilty, remembering the old song "Money is the root of all evil." In other words, they are muddled about money.

How does one sort out right from wrong? What does God say? For a start, God doesn't say that money is the root of all evil. The song misquotes the Bible. What it actually says is, "The love of money is the root of all evil," and that is a very different matter.

In the Bible, God has a lot to say about money, and much of it appears to be contradictory, because neither human beings nor the world are simple. The teaching needs to be looked at as a whole in order to get a balanced understanding of how God wants his people to live in this world.

He who is kind to the poor lends to the LORD, and he will reward him for what he has done.

Proverbs 19: 17

contents

Part 1
Blessings

Introduction Money was a relatively late idea—coins were not invented until about 600 BCE. Before that goods and services were acquired by bartering (exchanging other goods and services) and by weighing out pieces of silver and gold. It was all rather cumbersome, inexact, and open to fraud. The use of coins was fairer and much more efficient.

"I'm not interested in money," some people say, and think they mean it. But they're not being honest with themselves. "Money" is a way to speed up bartering. It means "goods and services," the important comforts and physical necessities of life.

The Bible is certainly interested in money, what money can buy, and what it can't buy. And so was Jesus. One-fifth of all he had to say was about money. And the first thing to be learned is that God says that in itself money is a blessing.

All good gifts

"God . . . richly provides us with everything for our enjoyment." 1 Timothy 6: 17

what the Bible has to say about:

money

Mark Water

DIMENSIONS
FOR LIVING
NASHVILLE

"*For where*

your treasure

is, there

your heart

will be also."

Luke 12: 34

This is a world of astonishing variety, complexity, and beauty, made by a God who "saw that it was good" (Genesis 1: 9, 12, 18, 21, 25). God is no killjoy. And money is a necessary part of this physical life. The words opposite were written in the context of advice about money.

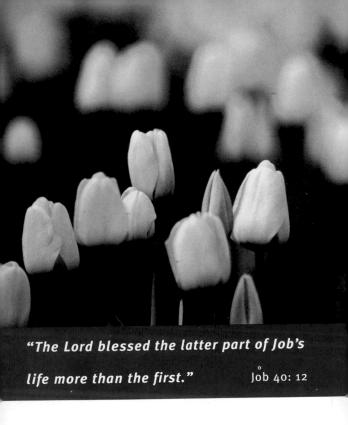

"The Lord blessed the latter part of Job's life more than the first."   Job 40: 12

A sign
of blessing

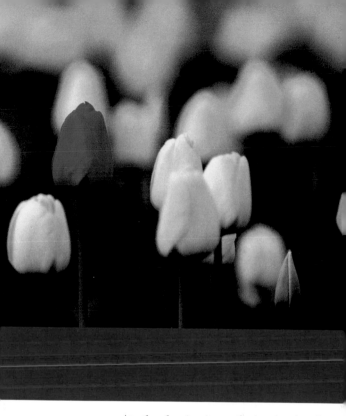

At the beginning of the book of Job, we read that Job had 7,000 sheep, 3,000 camels, 500 yoke of oxen, and 500 donkeys. At the end, Job had 14,000 sheep, 6,000 camels, 1,000 yoke of oxen, and 1,000 donkeys. The sign of God's blessing was the redoubling of Job's possessions.

The gift
of wealth

"Abram had become very

wealthy in livestock and in

silver and gold."

Genesis 13: 2

If poverty is good, why does God promise to eradicate it? Why give to the poor? God does sometimes call exceptional people to a life of poverty (John the Baptist, St. Francis of Assisi, Mother Teresa of Calcutta), but in the Bible the great men of faith (Abraham, Jacob, David, Solomon) were often men of wealth.

A good land

"You care for the land and water it; you enrich it abundantly . . . the valleys are mantled with grain; they shout for joy and sing."

Psalm 65: 9, 13

"I'm taking you away from here to a land flowing with milk and honey," God said to Moses when the Hebrews were slaves in Egypt. And sure enough, when Moses sent out spies to investigate this promised land, they came back laden with fruit. God's plan was for his people to live rich lives, materially as well as spiritually.

> *"The Lord God took the man and put him in the Garden of Eden to work it and take care of it."*
>
> Genesis 2: 15

The gift of work

"Thank God it's Friday" is the common refrain at the start of each weekend. Many people have an attitude problem where work is concerned. But that isn't how it was meant to be. God's plan is seen in the old story of Adam and Eve. Did they do nothing in the blissful Garden of Eden? No, they were gardeners.

Work and wealth

"Go to the ant, you sluggard; consider its ways and be wise! . . . it stores its provisions in summer and gathers its food at harvest." Proverbs 6: 6, 8

The Amish are known for their hard work and frugal Christian living; in April 2002 an article in the Wall Street Journal *reported that they are now very wealthy. In England, John Wesley spearheaded a religious revival among the poor working classes, which brought about a change in their fortunes. Many of those who lived by biblical principles became the well-off working classes.*

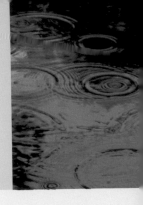

The blessing of giving

Paul was a tent maker, and wherever he went, he worked hard in order not to be a burden on the churches. And he gives a further reason for working hard: people earn money for the happiness of giving it away. To back up his point, Paul quotes this saying of Jesus—a saying that is not found in the Gospels.

"In everything I did, I showed you that by this kind of hard work we must help the weak, remembering the words the Lord Jesus himself said: 'It is more blessed to give than to receive.'"

Acts 20: 35

You think you know what God says (God's gift of work brings his gift of wealth), and then a seemingly contradictory principle leaps out. One day Peter came to Jesus with a cash-flow problem. And Jesus said, "Throw a line into the water, and you'll find a coin in the mouth of the first fish you catch."

A bigger picture

"The collectors of the two-drachma tax came to Peter and asked, 'Doesn't your teacher pay the temple tax?'"

Matthew 17: 24

Part 2
Warnings

Introduction George Best, the Irish soccer player, commented, "People say I wasted my money. I say 90 percent went on women, fast cars, and booze. The rest I wasted." But his ravaged face staring bleakly from the television screen tells a different story.

"Money often costs too much," said Ralph Waldo Emerson.

The United States has recently promised to give many billions of dollars to fight AIDS in South Africa. That money will do incalculable good. Many dream of all the good they could do, and the happiness they could bring, if they won the lottery. If they are aware of the teaching that the love of money is the root of all kinds of evil, they feel it doesn't really apply to them.

So what exactly is the cost that Emerson talked of? Why can wanting more cash be dangerous? Should coins, notes, and credit cards carry a spiritual health warning?

Suppose a man comes into your meeting wearing a gold ring and fine clothes, and a poor man in shabby clothes also comes in . . .

James 2: 1

28

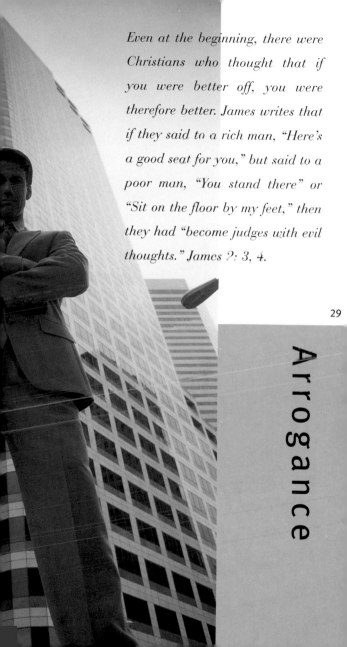

Even at the beginning, there were Christians who thought that if you were better off, you were therefore better. James writes that if they said to a rich man, "Here's a good seat for you," but said to a poor man, "You stand there" or "Sit on the floor by my feet," then they had "become judges with evil thoughts." James 2: 3, 4.

Arrogance

The one who received the seed that fell among the thorns is the man who hears the word, but the worries of this life and the deceitfulness of wealth choke it, making it unfruitful. Matthew 13: 22

"Man is a God-shaped blank," said Augustine. God should be at the center. But the thorns (wealth and worries) strangle God's life: here are the killing fields. In his parable about different types of ground, Jesus says that wealth is deceitful. Why is that? It's because people think it gives life, when in fact it gives lies.

The deceitfulness of wealth

Unreality

You lie on beds inlaid with ivory

and lounge on your couches.

You dine on choice lambs

and fattened calves.

Amos 6: 4

The fiery prophet railed against the Israelites because they were lounging around in luxury, eating expensive food, while all the time others were living in great poverty. Wealth tends to insulate people from reality and gives them a warped sense of priority.

Callousness

"*There was a rich man who was dressed in purple and fine linen and lived in luxury every day.*" Luke 16: 19

In Jesus' parable, a poor man
covered in sores lay at the rich
man's gate, hopelessly longing to
eat the leftovers from the table.
When death came, the rich man
was in misery in hell, while the
poor man was comforted in
heaven. Jesus isn't criticizing the
wealth of the rich man here.
He's condemning his cruelty.

Materialism

"It's a short step from wealth to materialism, from having riches to putting our trust in them," writes John Stott. "And many take it." And an offshoot of materialism is fear. Fear of having no money and therefore of being hungry, homeless, cold, or just plain empty inside, with no material satisfaction to fill the void.

Command those who are rich in this present world not . . . to put their hope in wealth, which is so uncertain, but to put their hope in God.

1 Timothy 6: 17

Watch out! Be on your guard against all kinds of greed; a man's life does not consist in the abundance of his possessions. Luke 12: 15

Fear leads to greed. Jesus followed up his warning words about greed with the story of the rich farmer who was planning to build larger barns in which to store his grain, and was looking forward to a comfortable retirement, when he suddenly died. God calls him a fool for thinking life is all about getting money.

Greed

Exploitation and injustice

. . . skimping the measure,

boosting the price and

cheating with dishonest

scales. Amos 8: 5

GREED" and people reel as whistle-blowers reveal the extent of corruption in big business. Giant pharmaceutical companies refuse to allow the manufacture of relatively cheap drugs for the millions who are dying in Africa. But it's easy to accuse others and to believe that big is worse. Seemingly tiny individual injustices are condemned by God.

Death

"Jesus said, 'Sell your possessions and give to the poor . . . then come, follow me.' When the young man heard this, he went away sad, because he had great wealth."

Matthew 19: 21, 22

The comedian Jack Benny joked that he was walking along when an armed robber came up and shouted, "Your money or your life!" There was a long pause. "Come on!" Jack replied. "Don't rush me. I'm thinking about it." That could never happen to us— could it? It happened to the rich young ruler. He walked away from eternal life.

Part 3
Looking

Introduction Margaret Thatcher, a former Prime Minister of the UK, has said, "A man who, after the age of thirty, finds himself on a bus can count himself a failure in life." By that reckoning, what does one make of Jesus, who at the age of 33 found himself on a cross?

One may argue that Jesus was different—and it's true, he was—but he also said to his friends, "Follow me."

Jesus turned many of the existing ideas about money upside down. To the amazement of the disciples, who thought that wealth was a sign of God's blessing, Jesus said, "How hard it is for the rich to enter the kingdom of God."

Jesus came to show us what God is like, so a good way of knowing what God says about money is by looking at the life of Jesus. And looking at Jesus, though it may not bring success by the world's standards, will bring prosperity to the soul.

Who, being in very nature God, did not consider equality with God something to be grasped, but made himself nothing, taking the very nature of a servant.

Philippians 2: 6, 7

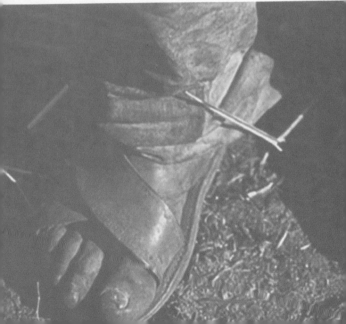

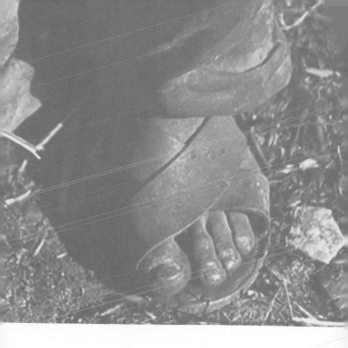

Letting go

*Jesus let go of the splendor
of heaven to become human,
to take on the obedience of a
slave. This is the antithesis of
arrogance. Then, having come
to this earth, he chose to live in
a (to the Jews) despised northern
village, in a (to the Romans)
despised tributary state.*

Jesus' home

Joseph and Mary went to Jerusalem to present him to the Lord . . . and to offer a sacrifice in keeping with what is said in the Law of the Lord: "a pair of doves or two young pigeons."   Luke 2: 22, 24

At Jesus' birth, Mary had to lay him in an animal feeding trough because Bethlehem was crowded out with visitors. Wouldn't you have chosen a palace for your son, or at least a rich home where he could have a good education and learn the refinements of life? When Mary and Joseph made the offering that was required after childbirth, they gave the offering that poor people were allowed to make.

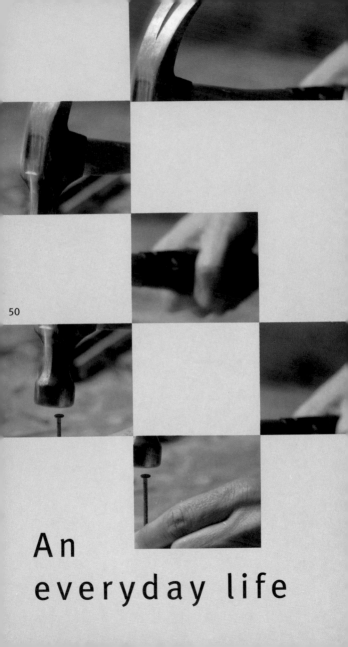

An
everyday life

Isn't this the carpenter's son?

Matthew 13: 55

Jesus' home was not wealthy, nor was it poverty-stricken. As the village builder and carpenter, Joseph was an important member of the community. It's likely that he died early on, and Jesus would then have taken over the family business. Until he was 30, Jesus worked in Joseph's carpentry shop.

At the age of 30, Jesus gave up financial security, choosing a life of real poverty. He had no paid job, no home of his own; he was an itinerant teacher who depended on the gifts of his friends. When Jesus talked about trusting God for daily provision, he was speaking from experience.

Jesus replied, "Foxes have holes and birds of the air have nests, but the Son of Man has no place to lay his head."   Luke 9: 58

Homelessness

Temptations

Then Jesus was led by the

Spirit into the desert to be

tempted by the devil . . . The tempter

came to him and said, "If you are

the Son of God, tell these stones to

become bread."   Matthew 4: 1, 3

The temptations reveal that in the wilderness Jesus was working out what it meant to carry out his mission as God's obedient Son. Jesus' first answer is a decisive refutation of materialism: "Man does not live on bread alone, but on every word that comes from the mouth of God." Matthew 4: 4.

Jesus' wealthy friends

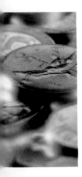

Zaccheus stood up and said to the Lord, "Look, Lord! Here and now I give half of my possessions to the poor, and if I have cheated anybody out of anything, I will pay back four times the amount." Luke 19: 8

When Zacchaeus made this surprise announcement, Jesus said, "Today salvation has come to this house." He didn't say, "That's not good enough, go and give the rest away, and then follow me." Jesus was not against money, only against dependence on money. Some of his followers were wealthy—how else could they have supported him and the 12 apostles?

Priorities

Jesus was in the process of teaching the crowds when this man jumped in with his request for Jesus to settle a family dispute over wills—a perennial problem. But Jesus would have none of it. Instead, he responded with a grave warning about the danger of greed.

59

"Teacher, tell my brother to divide the inheritance with me." Luke 12: 13

God first

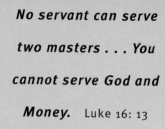

No servant can serve two masters . . . You cannot serve God and Money. Luke 16: 13

Jesus' life was all of a piece. He lived his teaching, though this led to actions that society thought unconventional, or even scandalous. When a woman poured expensive perfume over his head, people said, "This was worth a small fortune. It could have been sold and the money given to the poor." But Jesus saw deep love for God, and praised the woman.

Part 4
Giving

Introduction Christianity is the angel of heavenly mercy to the children of wretchedness, affliction, and woe. Or, at least, it should be. Throughout the ages we have seen individual Christians giving much more than a mere helping hand to the poor, oppressed, and suffering.

Emperor Constantine was the first to build hospitals for the sick and wounded in the provinces of the Roman Empire. William Wilberforce, after 40 years of struggle against vested interest in the English House of Commons, finally brought about the abolition of the slave trade in 1807. Mother Teresa won the Nobel Peace Prize in 1979 for her pioneering work among the dying on the streets of Calcutta.

Giving is not about money alone. It also includes time, skill, effort, expertise. It may mean simply spending two hours listening to someone in deep distress. But we cannot overlook the importance of money to bring about relief to those in need.

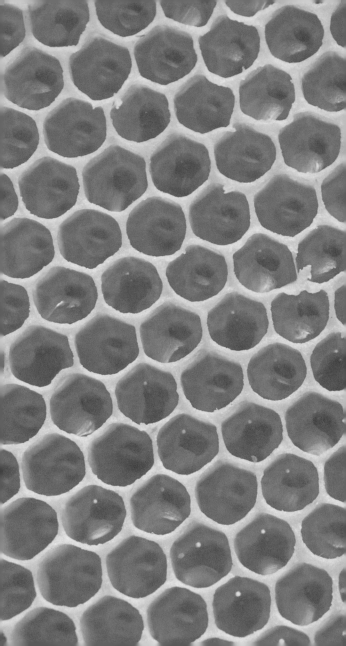

Communal lifestyle

All the believers were one in heart and mind. No one claimed that any of his possessions was his own, but they shared everything they had. Acts 4: 32

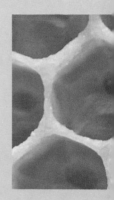

This has been hailed as the first experiment in "Christian communism." Some commentators point out that it was voluntary, and that the Christian community may have become poor because people sold their capital. However, there is much to admire here: their unity of purpose and their selflessness. It was truly a communion of saints.

A tithe of everything from the land, whether grain from the soil or fruit from the trees, belongs to the Lord; it is holy to the Lord.

Leviticus 27: 30

What is a tithe?

The tithe was a gift of 10 percent of one's crop production and animals, which was brought by God's people to the temple. The tithe was given to the Levites, who in turn gave 10 percent of it to the priests. Through the tithes, the people supported those who were engaged in maintaining the worship of God in Israel.

How often should I give?

On the first day of every week, each one of you should set aside a sum of money . . .

1 Corinthians 16: 2

A number of principles about giving can be gleaned from Paul's New Testament letters. In 1 Corinthians 16, the concept of regular giving is laid down. In this instance it is arranged on a weekly basis. A different pattern may be more convenient to others.

How much should I give?

. . . each one of you should set aside a sum of money in keeping with his income . . . 1 Corinthians 16: 2

Some people think that our giving should depend on our level of income. Others say that no specific details about this are given in the New Testament. Some have pointed out that 10 percent was the norm in the Old Testament, so we should give even more than that! The principle laid down here is that our giving should be proportionate to our income.

It's the attitude that counts

It is possible to be quite legalistic about how much money we will give back to God. That would be rather missing the point. For Christians are to be glad and happy, open and free, in their giving. We are to have "cheerful" hearts, not sullen, miserly interiors.

Each man should give what he has decided in his heart to give, not reluctantly or under compulsion, for God loves a cheerful giver.

2 Corinthians 9: 7

73

Giving locally

For the Scripture says, "Do not muzzle the ox while it is treading out the grain," and "The worker deserves his wages." 1 Timothy 5: 18

Should I support my local church? That is a matter of individual choice. But is it right that ministers of the gospel should live off the gospel? While Paul insisted that a laborer was worthy of his hire, he himself earned a living as a tent maker. In the Jewish tradition, however, it was accepted that priests were paid by the people.

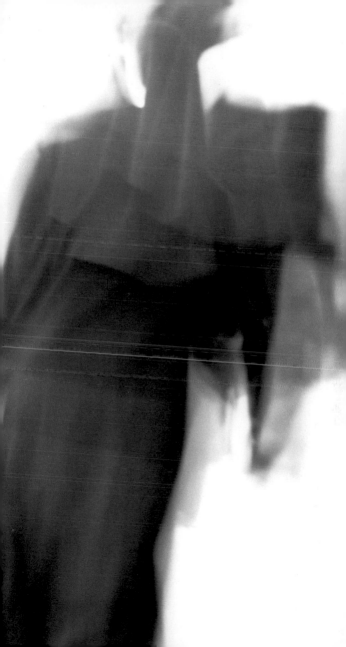

Disasters and famines outside our immediate locality should concern us—our giving should extend beyond the frontiers of our own country. As he traveled around the Roman Empire, Paul spent a good deal of his time making a collection of money for people in special need back in Jerusalem.

Supporting

Now about the collection for

God's people.

1 Corinthians 16: 1

other churches

"If anyone has material possessions and sees his brother in need but has no pity on him, how can the love of God be in him?"

1 John 3: 17

A needy brother

One of the greatest privileges that rich Christians have is the joy of sharing their material possessions with people in need. But the apostle John is writing here to prick the conscience of Christians who had the means to help the poor, but would not lift a finger to do so. Such Christians are kidding themselves if they think they love God.

What he sold will remain in the possession of the buyer until the Year of Jubilee. It will be returned in the Jubilee, and he can then go back to his property. Leviticus 25: 28

Built into the laws of the Old Testament was the Year of Jubilee, held every 50th year, when anyone who had been forced to sell his family property was given it back. All slaves and prisoners were also released. This unique system of social justice, if it had been followed, would have eliminated poverty.

Justice
and
poverty

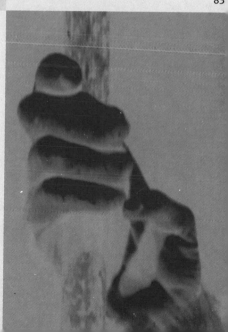

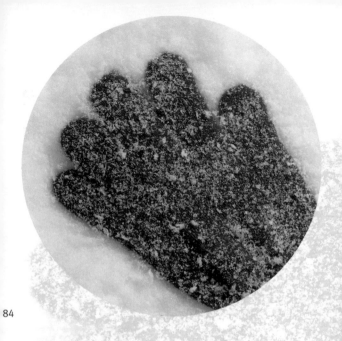

Faithfulness

"His master replied,
'Well done, good and
faithful servant! You have
been faithful with a few
things; I will put you in
charge of many things.'"

Matthew 25: 23

In Jesus' parable of the talents it is the faithfulness of two of the men that is commended. The man who had five talents and the man who had two receive equal commendation. For what is necessary in any steward is that he is found to be faithful. Christians are to make full use of their gifts and talents, including their money.

Stocks and

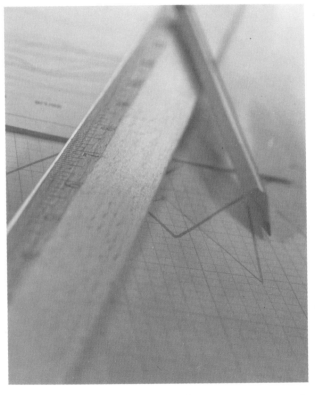

shares?

. . . whatever you do, do it all for the glory of God. 1 Corinthians 10: 31

There are countless ethical considerations in connection with money and wealth. What is a reasonable standard of living for a Christian to aspire to or possess? Is it right to invest on the stock market? How much should I save? The guiding principle to hang on to is that everything should be done for the glory of God.

Into debt?

The rich rule over the poor, and the borrower is servant to the lender. Proverbs 22: 7

Is it wrong to be in debt? How else can one ever buy a car, let alone a home? The Bible never says that debt in itself is wrong. It just has timely warnings about the dangers of debt. It can all too easily become the slippery road to financial ruin.

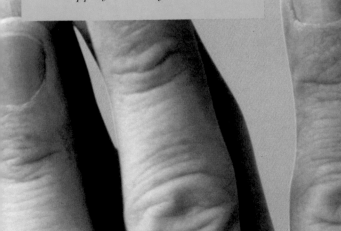

Bribes

"Do not accept a bribe, for a bribe blinds those who see and twists the words of the righteous."

Exodus 23: 8

There are certain activities that the Bible categorically states should not be indulged in. Taking a bribe and offering bribes are very much a way of life in certain businesses and in certain countries. It is not always easy to say no to a bribe. Christians, however, are told not to take bribes.

Generosity is the key

Remember this: Whoever sows sparingly will also reap sparingly, and whoever sows generously will also reap generously. 2 Corinthians 9: 6